I0422911

FIRST STEPS

A
Young Adult
Help Book

Revised Edition

by

Anne M. Angell

First Steps

Dear Young Adult:

Congrats! Either you are headed to being a graduate or you graduated already. So, more than likely, you are now 18, or soon to be one. That is the magic number that teens wait for. It means you are officially an adult.

Just to help you get in the right perspective for this book, I'd like you to imagine yourself standing in your home, facing the front door. Now, open the door and take a step outside. What do you see?

When I tutored Math to young adults, their last time with me, I asked the same question. I never got the response I was hoping for. They usually said the trees, lawn, a car, the neighbor across the street, etc. So, I tried to open their imagination. To be a successful adult, you must open your imagination up and see above and beyond. Whether you are an overachiever or an underachiever, it doesn't matter. All it takes is someone who can see more than what is before their eyes.

So, now, see this as you open the door and take a step outside: the whole world at your feet. From the plains, mountains, oceans, seas, rivers and valleys, from New York to Singapore, Alaska to South Africa, the world is before you. The adventure begins in your mind and if you set it high enough and broad enough, you can do anything and go anywhere. You have plenty of years to get it right, so relax.

One step out into the world is all it takes. You don't have to be the one that only dreams ; you can be the one that makes the dream a reality. How far

you go and what you do rests with you. Don't ever let anyone say, "You can't." You can do what they only dreamed about and others have achieved.

Being an adult means responsibility, with accountability, and becoming a productive participant in life. At the same time, it is an adventure that never has to end. Blaming your parents, others, the school, your life for where you are at this point becomes pointless. From this point on, you are the so-called Captain of your own ship. Either you set the course for calm seas, peace and tranquility. Or, you steer your life into open waters of turbulence, much anguish and pain, and disappointment.

I wrote this book to help you make a smooth transition into the every-day experiences that will begin to become a part of your new life as an adult.

I hope you find it a helpful tool and I wish you all the best.

Now, close your eyes, take in a deep breath, and expel it out as you open your eyes. Take the first step into a world with endless possibilities.

Sincerely,

Pam

First Steps

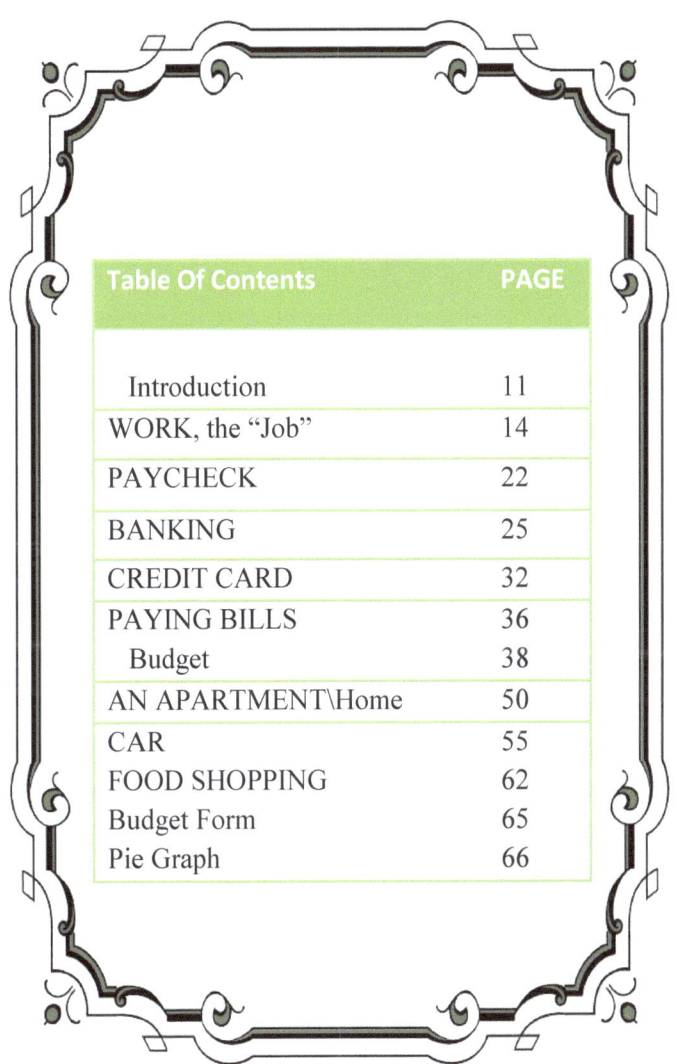

Table Of Contents	PAGE

INTRODUCTION

Well, although teachers are almost a thing of the past, old books are burned or returned, and most of your friends have gone their separate ways, you, still, have to face the future. Don't dive right in; wade in the low end first. Get a feel for what you can expect.

Most may be contemplating college. Sadly, many think of this time as Party On! Instead of work—work, and more work, you need time for a serious contemplation on the future. Many delay the future as they relish their first experience of freedom. Freedom from parental control, the do this and don't do that, day in and day out— rules . . . rules and more rules. Well, we all like to take the moment to dream. So, take it now, because tomorrow reality will hit you square in the face. Parents are exchanged for the laws of the land. You think they had dos and don'ts, wait until you face the real world. Dos and don'ts follow you everywhere you go: stores, streets, buildings, hospitals, college, the work place, etc. The best way to keep on the right side and stay out of trouble is just cooperate. It is that simple. Being in the world isn't about being selfish. Those days as a teen, being selfish, are over. It is time to fit in and, hopefully, contribute to the well being and peace of the land. You aren't supposed to be the problem; you are to become the solution.

At one time, I used to tutor Math to young teens. One of the first things I learned is they thought they knew what to expect once out of school, but they really didn't. So, at the end of the school year, I gave them a few notes to help them know what to anticipate later in life. In this book, I am taking the same premise and stretching the idea to include as many obstacles as a young man or woman might face in life. Like a new colt out of the gate, you can expect some

hurdles to jump. Hopefully, this book can prepare you for what awaits you.

I'd say the first thing to expect is how you *present* yourself to others in the real world. By this I mean, in the workplace, stores, church, and society in general, do you act more mature and confident through your words, actions, and appearance? You are a packaged deal inside and out. The outside is all many have to make a quick evaluation and judgment on what is on the inside of a person. It's like a mental snapshot.

As a teen, ones odd behavior was tolerated for no other reason than you were a teen. People expect certain behavior from a teen and, although not all of it is especially liked, it is tolerated to a degree. However, as a new-functioning citizen of the land, your behavior can determine how far you go in life. Certain behavior isn't tolerated from an adult. In fact, it is frowned upon. Do adults act like immature brats? Some do. Does it make it right? Never. Adults are always supposed to set the standard of right and good and be the example to follow. Learn from their mistakes, or your own for that matter, and don't repeat them.

Just know that every time you learn something new, you take that into your next experience. Let's say you go to the Courthouse to deal with your taxes and they want certain forms and identification, but you didn't have them. Well, next time you go, you are aware and better prepared for a similar situation. You find out what is needed before you go. It saves time; grief and frustration are not involved.

Many things can be done over the internet, which saves time and effort. Most states have a site that can walk you through most important aspects of things pertaining to the government, for instance: your taxes, titles, licenses, social security, phone numbers to local government offices, etc. Use as many of these as possible. Become one of the informed ones.

Don't always run to your parents. Learn to solve issues for yourself. Sooner or later, you're going to have to do it anyway. Learn to be resourceful, informed, aware, knowledgeable about important life issues, and learn to be productive, not counterproductive.

When you come to a roadblock and you've done all you can think to do, then come to your parents for advice or help. Tell them what you did first to resolve an issue and see what advice they can offer. Show them you are maturing, by your being forthright and resourceful. Ignorance is not about knowing something. You become ignorant, if you never ask. The old saying is true, "They've been there, done that, and have the bumper sticker and tee shirt to prove it." Every adult started where you are today. Always know that they are there to help you every step of the way.

WORK, the "Job"

Employer: the one you work for . . . the Boss
Employee: the worker on the job, who works for the company or Employer

Qualifications

Many young adults believe they are qualified to do anything. When you go for that first job, you must be honest with yourself. Can you do the work required by your knowledge and skills? Are you willing to learn and be assertive? Are you willing to give the business what they need, the hours required, and the best quality of work they demand (ask\need)? A business can only function by the product going out of it. When you work for a company, you become a part of their success or failure. If you give them poor output, it reflects on them. Who wants to purchase an inferior product or labor? People want the best and that must be your mentality as well.

Sadly, today, many give the company below-standard work, as few hours as possible. Yet, they cry when their paycheck isn't on time. A company expects from you eight hours of your best work. Not eight hours of seeing how little you can get by with, yet expect eight hours of pay. This mentality will end your so-called career speedily. That mentality leaves a poor paper trail on your resume, which will follow you: Fired! Late for work. Always taking breaks or hiding in the lunch room or bathroom. Calls in sick a lot. Can't get to work, car always breaking down. Got hurt on the job *again*.

Whatever you left behind from the last job is noted by the next Employer. Make sure it is always a good report and recommendation.

You need to prepare a **resume**: an overall view of your experience, skills, where you have been, and what you have done. This is the opportunity to convince a hiring manager that you have the needed skills to bring to the position. This is the time to impress them. If you are right out of school, then offer them what you did in school, or extracurricular activities. An **objective** means: Why are you applying for the job? What is the type of career you are looking for? Saying you want to utilize your skills of cutting grass, landscaping, and knowledge of plants wouldn't be appropriate if you went to a business that sells clothes. No match exists.

If a company wants to see your **resume** and you show them a list of jobs you have been in and out of for a year, they will question what the problem is with you. Most people work a steady job for a long period of time, meaning years. If you worked over three or four jobs in less than a year, it reflects poorly on you. The only reasonable excuse they might accept is that you moved a lot within the state or country. Even then, they want to know why you moved around often. Why is this important? Who wants to take the time and show an Employee the ropes, and within a short time, knowing they might be out the door? It wastes their time. If you are such a person, they won't consider you. You could be a liability, not an asset. A company that is hiring is looking for a reliable, steady person who plans to be with them for a long period of time. As an example, an **apprentice**. Many opportunities exist where a company is willing to teach a skill (a trade) to a newcomer. For instance a plumber, carpenter, electrician, etc.

If your excuse for all the jobs you left are: "Didn't like them," the boss didn't like you, you were misunderstood; they *worked* you too hard, the hours didn't allow you to have any social interaction, or

worse, they fired you, then I can almost guarantee they will not be running to the phone to ask you for another interview. All you, simply, relayed to them is you were lazy, incompetent, unyielding, a complainer, weak, and unwilling to give them your best effort.

Here is reality: Most people need to work. Starting out, you, probably, don't have much to offer a business\company. They can overlook your inexperience, if you can prove to them that you are the *Best*, because you will go above and beyond what they need or are asking from you. You are the Go-Getter and all they can see is their business thriving, growing, and building into a fine-successful business, because they hired you. You must prove your worth. Yes; even at a fast-food restaurant. A lot, and I mean a lot, of successful people started at the bottom and worked their way up. Don't sneer at small beginnings.

Like what you are doing

If you don't like it, than it will become drudgery. If it is drudgery, your work will show it. Is it something you can picture yourself doing twenty years from now? Look around and imagine yourself working in that environment. Is it something that seems pleasing, or do you feel it is something that you couldn't tolerate? Or, do you see it as a stepping-off place and so you are willing to give your best to have a good beginning to your career? Someone in the mailroom can eventually land a job in one of the offices. From there, it depends on how far they want to go to succeed. A company is more apt to hire someone inside the company that knows them and are qualified to do the job, than seek out someone who they have to start over with. Just because you are in the mailroom, doesn't mean the Executives weren't paying attention to the quality of work you do and your work ethics. Remember; they talk in the lunchroom, too. Remember, too. If you do not like the job, do not blame them and return your loathing back on them by poor-quality work. They need that position filled, whether you like it or not. Leave, so they can get someone in who wants to work that job. They are giving you an exchange for your work: a pay check. No matter what, give them your best.

Once on the job, glean from the veterans. Learn what worked for them or didn't. Here is a good place to learn good work ethics. Watch and observe. Each job you get, you can take a skill or knowledge with you. It builds character and teaches you what works and doesn't work. Nothing on the job is insignificant. Those who are successful are, usually, more than responsive to give you good-sound advice to help you succeed. Listen and learn. Just because school is over and the books are put away does not mean learning ends. In fact, you will learn and discover new things for the rest of your life. Absorb it all, because you never know when it will help you out later in life.

The Job Interview

The economy isn't in the best of shape. People with experience, skills, knowledge, and degrees have a better chance of getting that job you are applying for than you do. Don't get discouraged . . . get wise. This isn't the time to walk into your first-job interview, or even the first appearance, to fill out an application looking like something that the cat drug in off the street. First appearance and behavior could mean you landing a job or your application being filed in the trash. Your clothes should always be conservative, clean, and tidy. Your first appearance is your signature; who you are as a person. Nails and hair clean and kept. If you walk in like a hood, like you're all that, you can expect to be a big question mark on their mind, a risk. No one wants to work with someone who looks threatening or untrustworthy. Never count on the discrimination card. All that tells them is you will be trouble and rough waters ahead for them.

Leave the arrogant attitude at the door. Walk in confident, shoulders back, head held high, with a smile of enthusiasm, not cockiness. Don't act like they are there to cater to you; act like you want to cater to them. Even the receptionist and your attitude toward them are not overlooked by the Employer. Slouching in the chair will make you appear lazy, bored easily, with an I-don't-care attitude. If you appear this way now, they will wonder how you will work for them later when on the job. Many believe their attitude and behavior are not important these days, especially if you apply at a fast-food restaurant, grocery store, or retail store. Most believe these will hire anyone, because they are glad (*desperate*) to get anyone they can. Again, it is a business and a business cannot survive without **customers**. **No** customers, **no** revenue; **no** revenue, **no** paycheck; **no** paycheck, eventually, **no** job. They went out of business.

All this can spiral downward, if you or the employees do not do their part to contribute to the growth of the business. They need customers. And, if your behavior and attitude scares these potential customers away (who came in to spend money), you can be shown quickly to the door. (Their spent money is your paycheck!) The more you please a customer, the more they are apt to buy, or return to the business, sometimes because they want to do business with only YOU. This shows the Employer you are valuable to them and they want to keep you as an **asset**.

Many know they aren't qualified for the job, so they pull the discrimination card out. They feel the company has to hire them, because any form of discrimination isn't tolerated. Becoming successful depends on you and how you view yourself. If you get a job for no other reason than your appearance, then you, by your own actions, relayed your own worth. Come on; start out life with the right attitude.

Make sure you have basic information available to fill out the application: address, date of birth, birthplace, Social Security

Number, schools attended, graduation date, just to name a few. They want dates from previous Employers. They are going to want to know what skills you had to use on that job. If you are right out of school, they are interested in what you did in school, like: sports, extracurricular activities, drama, music, etc. These define you as someone who went above and beyond what was required of a student. Grades are important, too. Spell correctly! Print legibly!

When in the interview, introduce yourself with a good-firm handshake, a clean hand. Always use Mr. So-and-So or if female, Ms. **Miss** means single; **Mrs.** means married, and **Ms.** means Miss or Mrs., so it is proper etiquette to use Ms. if not sure. Many do not like to be called, "Ma'am", because it denotes *old*. No one likes to seem old, even if they look 80. **Never** use their first name, unless they say to use it. More likely than not, many during the introduction will tell you what to call them, so pay attention and listen.

Sit up straight. This is not the time to display any bad, gross, or unusual behavior.

At the end of the interview, smile, shake their hand, and thank them for this opportunity. Leave them with a good impression about you.

Behavior on the job:

At first, no one minds you asking how things are done. In fact, it is expected. What gets you into trouble, or in bad standing, is when you ask the same question days even weeks after you were hired. Within two to three weeks of being on most jobs, a person should know how and what they are expected to do. If not, a problem exists with your ability to comprehend and follow through with instructions. It is for you to find out why you are weak in these areas. Fix it before you are pulled into the office.

- Don't bring your issues and problems to work.

- Don't divulge everything about yourself the first few days or ever.
- Stay positive and cheerful
- Don't be underfoot
- Don't find places to hide to get out of work. Trust me. It is being observed and recorded, even if it is in the boss's memory.
- Don't keep looking at the clock and asking when work is over.
- Do not come in reeking of drugs or alcohol and do not bring them to work. Worse, do not sell drugs at work, even in the parking lot.

Remember; these days, security cameras are everywhere. So, slipping your hand in the till, sneaking food out that was meant for the customer, stuffing merchandise in your pocket, going behind their backs, doing inappropriate or disgusting behavior in secret, etc., it is caught on tape. Again, is this how you want others to see you? A thief, liar, cheat, repulsive individual, deceiver. . . . Temptations are everywhere. That doesn't mean you have to *act* upon a one. Be better than that.

The boss, manager, the one above you, they are in charge; you are not. No one minds suggestions, but few like to be told what to do. You have a problem, if you cannot follow orders (or policy). Find out their policy and follow it.

Protocol is in place for a reason. Don't step outside the bounds of them.

Do the work you were hired to do and always give out your best.

The right Job:
Be careful and don't get a job that will eat up most of your money in gas, because you have to drive far. Or, one that it costs you

in buying lunches every day. These eat away your income and quickly.

Find a job that has "perks" that can benefit you in the long run. This includes: Medical Insurance, 401K, share of profit, etc. Although your hourly wage may be small, these **benefits** are income and can save you out-of-pocket monies in the long run. They are like pay\income.

Make sure your personality doesn't clash with the Employer or Employees. Fighting on the job, which causes you to hit someone (proof of your character and weaknesses), is an assault—a crime. Always keep your emotions in check, learn self control in all areas, and bring all issues you have to those who are in charge. Committing a crime or being sued isn't the best way to begin your new life as an adult.

NOTE: See page 48 ▸▸ . . . ◂◂

PAYCHECK

You have the job, so you have a paycheck. Your Paycheck is your **Income**. Your willingness to succeed determines your income, the amount you live off of every day. Most people get paid every week. Some get paid bi-weekly. This means 26 paychecks a year.

The typical deductions from your paycheck that you can expect are: Federal Income Tax, Social Security, State, Local, or city Taxes. Others can be the 401K, contribution to medical insurance, opted portion for investment, etc.

To make it easy to always know what you will take home after a week of hard work, I suggest: Divide by three into the weekly total and subtract a third from the total. This will always give you the average of what to expect—**take-home pay**. It can be a little above or below, but it will be close enough for you to make a quality decision on how much money you will have by the end of the week or month.

EXAMPLE:

So, let's say you make $7.00 an hour: **hourly wage**. Most work 40 hours a week. So, 40 X 7 = 280. Your earnings will be $280 for a week's work. Now, divide 3 into 280, which is 93.33, or $93. So, $280 - $93 = $187. The whole paycheck will be approximately $187 take-home pay. **Take-home pay** is what you will have for yourself to spend or save. Or, $748 for the month ($187 X 4 = $748).

Another example: $10 an hour and you work 45 hours. 45 X 10 = 450 ÷ 3 = 150 – 450 = approximately $300 take-home pay for the week. Or, $300 X 4 (weeks in a month) = $1,200 a month.

<u>Another example</u>: $10 X 40 = $400 ÷ 3 = 133 − 400 = $266.67 for the week. Or, $1,066.68 a month to spend.

For a long time, it was your parent's responsibility to foot the bills for you: providing a place to live, food, clothes, activities, etc. Those days are coming to an end. It's time to know what to expect in the real world.

At first, $748 or $1,067 may sound like a lot of money. Or, is it? Sure, if you stayed home and allowed your parents to provide and continue to take care of you, while you did with your money what you wanted; it could seem like a lot. (If anything, this is the time to save for your future.) As you experience paying bills, you are going to learn why your parent's couldn't always afford that had-to-have item on the spur of the moment when you wanted it. You will see firsthand what they have gone through to make sure you had a roof over your head, food on the table, and clothes to wear. And, sure, some of you didn't get that much. Entering the real world, you will understand just why they struggled.

You don't want to just get by; you want to exceed and to excel in whatever you do. You want this for yourself and lastly for your family, which will follow soon enough. If you can't provide for you, how will you provide for others: wife and children?

Other means of a Paycheck:

An **hourly wage** is what the company pays you by the hour.

Commission means you may get a small wage per hour, but the *bulk* of your income must come by what you sell. A Commission is, usually, found in sales jobs\positions. So, make sure you understand this when you apply. Your commission is determined by how much you sell by your effort.

Tips: A waitress\waiter, bus boy, or matradee (maitre d') live off of their tips. Each place of business is different, so make sure you

are aware of the consequences involving your pay. Some offer a minimum hourly rate and it is your responsibility for the tips (your income\pay). Bad attitude, laziness, and bad habits will not influence a customer to give you a big tip. A 15% tip is customary on the pre-taxed order. So, if the customer's dinner was $30, it would be: $30 x .15 = $4.50 (tip).

As you will, soon, learn in many companies, performance is everything. You treat a customer crappy, than a commission isn't likely, or a tip. The customer is your Employer, in a sense.

FACT: The average family lives on about, or less than, $45,000 a year. Both adults working, it can be over $65,000. Below $20,000, you are getting close to poverty level, meaning you will struggle to make it and get far in life or success. My view, an income between $22,000 to $35,000, a person can live comfortably, **if** they are careful about what they spend.

Let's break it down, so you have an idea of the hourly income you will want to aim for:

<u>**Total year's income at $45,000**</u>

$45,000 ÷ 12 (months a year) = $3,750 a month; 3,750 ÷ 4 (weeks a month) = $937.50 a week; $937.50 ÷ 40 (hours a week) = **$23.44**— *the hourly wage*. This is the amount you need to aim for to be able to provide for your family, have a home, and a car.

And, don't forget, to budget accurately with this figure, you need to divide it by 3 (taxes and deductions). So, $45,000 ÷ 3 = $15,000

$45,000 - $15,000 = $30,000

$30,000 ÷ 12 = <u>$2,500</u> a month *figure to budget with*

$2,500 ÷ 4 = $625 a week

$625 ÷ 7 (days a week) = $89.30 a day

BANKING

Now that you have a paycheck, you shouldn't cash it and carry it around in your pocket. Let's just say it isn't the wisest thing to do. It's time to find a bank and establish better credit. Look for a bank that can be utilized in most states. You never know when you are out-of-town and you need the assistance of a bank: to cash a check, use the ATM without a hefty charge, use a Notary without any cost, etc. For now, you might want to stick to simple-banking practices. It is wise to get a checking and a savings account.

A **checking account** is where you put your hard-earned money. You can draw from that money; it is yours. Some banks require a certain amount to be established in the account, so you are not charged fees. To open an account, you need some money to put in there, sometimes as little as $50.

Fees are expenses from the bank <u>for services</u> they provide. If you keep a high enough amount in their bank, many of them wave these fees. Each bank is different, so check around and ask.

With a checking account, you get checks. **Checks** are a contract. Once you put your signature on the check, it is binding. It is saying that you have X amount of money in your checking account and you are assuring the person on the receiving side that they will get their money for the goods or services they provided. The bank is not the responsible party! You are. They are the middle man that makes sure the contract is honored and the transaction is followed through expediently. So, never blame the bank for funds not being there. Writing checks that *you know* lack the necessary funds is an illegal action. These are called, **bad checks**, or bounced check.

Checks are a contract and if a breach in the contract occurs, you can run into legal problems.

Checks, with a false signature on it (not your signature), is known as a **forged check**. This, too, is an illegal act. So, do not leave your checks out where anyone can get to them and use them.

You use checks the same as you would cash. Understand that once you hand over the check, it does take a while before the check is cashed. Once you write the check, as far as you are concerned, that money is **spent**. Whosever's name is on the check, that is their money, not yours. Although you may see the money in your account, un-cashed, for a period of time, never use it; it is gone because you gave it over to someone. I've had a check go un-cashed for over six months. It turned out the person lost it behind their microwave. It used to be, and may still be the rule, but checks were deemed null and void once a year was up, from the exact date on the check. So, if it was May11, 2000 when you put the date on the check; it is good until May 11, 2001. The only problem with someone not cashing the check is it messes your records up, because that amount continues to be outstanding in your account.

If you ever write a check and make a mistake on it, make sure you write in bold-large print the word across the check: VOID. Tear up the check into small pieces. Again, it is a legal-binding contract and you don't want someone using the signed check for their own personal gain.

When you write a check, the business will want to see a driver's license, a form of ID, and, sometimes, they ask for a social security number.

A **Savings Account** is an account that holds your money that you want to save for a later date. It is over and above the left over monies after paying the bills. You need a good, safe place to put your extra monies. Sooner or later, you can begin to set money aside and watch it accumulate. Again, you determine the growth. It is your money to do with as you please. Make sure that you check with the Bank to see if you must maintain a certain amount in the account. A fee might be involved and, sometimes, the monthly fee can eat away your savings. A savings account can earn interest. These days, however, it isn't a whole lot, so don't get too excited. Still, a penny is a penny. Years ago, it wasn't unusual to see a few dollars added to your savings every month. Now, you are lucky to see it ever come close to ten cents. No matter what the interest is; the savings can be a good place to keep your money, and also, help you from spending it, like impulse buying. Out of sight; out of mind\pocket.

Interest: a percentage on a total amount, added to your funds. EX: $100 savings with a promised 2% interest = 100 x .02 = $2 You, now, have $102 in your savings.

Paying Bills

Today, we have many means to pay our bills. I, personally, like the on-line banking. It is fast, no mailings, a 24\7 quick glance at what I have in all accounts. I can see what bills need paid, when they were paid, and how much I have left over to spend. I can do all this with a push of a button. No checks, no hassle, no stamps and envelops to lick; it is fast and convenient. It is my first recommendation. To establish on-line banking, all you need is to put in your account information, decide a log-on name, and a good password. Write down the sign in name and password and put them in a safe place, in case you forget them. Only you should know what it is. Never give out any of this information, even to a close friend.

To pay a bill online, all you need to do is find the section that says, Pay Bills. Put in the information for the person, business, or organization that you owe money to and the account is established. Once established, all you have to do is put in an amount owed them,

push the button, and the transaction is taken care of. Some businesses, like Cable or Utilities, can get the funds within a day or two. Others, it may take up to five to seven days.

However, if you do choose to use checks to pay bills, I have one strong warning: Don't use the statement or ATM amount to determine what your **actual cash value** is, at that time.

Here is why: You have $300 in your checking. You added your paycheck of $375. Now, your total is $675. You paid your monthly bills *with checks*, which came to $425. That leaves you with **$250**. A few days later, you go to the ATM machine to see what is in your balance. You see that you have **$385** in the checking account. You get excited, because you just saw something you wanted to purchase for $275. You buy the item. A few days later, the bank informs you that a check bounced. **Bounced** means, it went to the bank, the bank saw no funds, and returned the bad check to the business. The contract was broken. The merchant can charge you a hefty fee (sometimes up to $50, so beware!) for re-writing another check. Now, you are irate. You blame the bank. No; you forgot that a mailed check takes days to arrive at the merchant, it takes them a while to deposit the check, and then a few more days before your bank can complete the transaction by releasing the funds from your account to the businesses to pay the bills. The ATM or monthly statement can only show what they *see*, or what transactions took place. They can't *see* a check going through the mailing system and they aren't aware you even wrote a check. Their ESP powers are not working, when it comes to you writing checks. This is why the checks come with a ledger, a credit and debit booklet for your records. You need to post each transaction with the amount and date. ▶ If you are keeping an accurate account ledger, then this is what you need to rely upon to know the exact amount in your account, not the ATM.

Another thing to add into the equation is this mistake many have made. If the bank does charge a monthly fee of, let's say, $5.00, you can't overspend and deplete the monies needed for the fee. You *know* the fee is part of the banking process (no surprise), so don't spend what is theirs rightfully. Some people like to live on the edge and they don't keep a lot of monies in their account. As an example, it is getting to the end of the month and the statements are being prepared. You have $7.50 in your account. You wrote a check at a convenient store for $4.23. The bank draws out their $5.00 monthly fee and you learn later that another fee was added, because of the discrepancy. Again, it wasn't their fault.

Credit: plus monies
Debit: negative monies (red: negative amount, below $0)

$7.50 [+ credit]
$4.23 (check [- debit]) + $5 (bank fee) [- debit] = $9.23
$9.23 (- debit) - $7.50 (+ credit) = $1.73 (-debit)

As you can see, you didn't leave enough in your checking to compensate for all the debits.

I have always done this when I used checks (I do everything online, now.) and it never failed me. I put a hidden amount into my checking that I never touched (spent) or used in my monthly calculations. It is $500. So, even if I messed up, I have the $500 to back up my mistake. And, yes; the bank has a system, too. But I, personally, like my method better. It keeps my records, paper trail, clean. No bounced checks, no extra fees. The bank has their method: **Over-Draft Protection**. This is like insurance. They will compensate for your mistake, by providing the funds. This gives you time to get the appropriate funds in your account to cover the charge. Check their monthly-fee amount. Without it, a $4 burger could cost

you $35 for an **overdraft** (no monies to cover expense in your account) on your credit card.

The bank is always willing to help you with any of your financial concerns. If you keep a good record, you can never lose unnecessary monies, because of poor choices and preventable mistakes.

If you are ever given a check, on the back, an area with a line across from it exists on the end. Never sign the check, until you are at the bank and ready to cash it or put into your account. If you ever sign the check before that and someone finds it, they can cash it. Mistakes happen and it could slip by someone who isn't doing their job by checking for proper identification. The check is a contract. Once your signature is on the back, the transaction is legal and binding and can be cashed. More often than not, you can't cash the check unless it is in your own bank. Or, use the bank where the check was written from. Or, you can go to a Check-Cashing Business and they will cash the check. BEWARE: these charge a hefty fee for this service and can eat up to a third of your check.

A check is like cash. So, you don't want it in a place where it can be easily taken.

Using an ATM

ATM (Automated Teller Machine) is a means to get cash, deposit a check(s), and check on your balances, without having to go into the bank. You are issued a card that can draw the monies out and to take care of your personal business.

If you are ever out of town and want cash, ★be aware that using another bank's ATM that isn't from your bank, an extra charge can be applied. (For instance, your bank is Chase and the other bank is Bank Atlanta.) As an example: You withdrawal $20. The fee for using the machine at Bank Atlanta with a Chase card is $2.50 and the bank charges at Chase Bank is $2.50. That is a fourth of the $20. You may hold a twenty, but it cost you five dollars to get $20 from an outside bank, other than Chase. Ouch. This goes back to why I said it is wise to use a bank that is established in most states, in case you travel.

CREDIT CARD

Now, you have a job, you have a paycheck, and you established a good bank and banking practices. You are on your way. I am sure you want to spend some of that money. A credit card is one way to buy\purchase items.

Many forms of credit cards exist. Simply, they are a means to purchase an item without money. Don't get too excited. You do have to pay it all back. I think that is why so many have astronomical, credit-card debt. Somewhere, in their mixed logic, they didn't think they had to pay it back (out of sight; out of mind). So, it mounted into a sizeable debt, a debt many struggle to pay off. It comes back to NEED or WANT. Don't spend what *you know* you can't pay back right away.

Loan: an institution is giving you a set amount of money, to use, but it must be paid off. It, usually, comes with interest. This is borrowed money.

A credit card is like a loan. Most credit card institutions have a set amount that you can't go over. For instance, you can get a card for $2,500. So, you can't spend more than that amount. It is a $2,500 credit to you, as if you had $2,500. Don't get too excited. It is money that is loaned and it does have to be paid back. Most institutions determine how much they will risk on you by your income and your FICO score (see page 49). Like I said before, you are leaving a paper trail behind you, so make sure it is always a good trail.

The amount they are willing to risk can be determined by your assets. **Assets** (+) are anything that has value: a house, property, jewelry, a car, investments, etc. Assets are the plus (credit) side of your worth or monetary value. The more assets, the better you look on paper. Until you cash them in, they are *objects* of value. You could purchase a ring for $5,000 and think you had $5,000 worth of assets. But, it sold for only $3,500. The actual value of the asset was the **cash value**. Many things are determined by the **cash value**, not by what you paid for the item. This holds true with a brand-new vehicle. Sure, you just bought it for $20,000. Once you drove it off the lot, its value dropped.

Debit Card: This is a card that you can use to take out cash or make a purchase by using your actual cash value in the bank. The amount is determined by the amount in your checking account. The transaction is instant and comes out of your checking account.

Credit Card: As I said, it has a set limit and is like a loan and has an interest rate. Each month, you will see on the statement what you spent and the amount of interest accrued (accumulated) on the debt. Beware; the more risk a company takes on you, the higher the interest rate can be, up to 28%, or more, sometimes well over a fourth of the actual purchased price. If you pay off the amount you spent, you will never see any interest. The accrued amount is added to the next statement and if you never make a large enough payment to pay off the debt, it keeps getting bigger (Purchase [Principal amount] + Interest + accrued interest from last month). Each company charges interest in a different way. Read the contract and fine print, ask questions, and make sure you understand what kind of card you are getting, what to expect, and their policy on the interest rate.

Accrued Expenses are expenses you have not paid for and they accumulate, because you add onto them. **Accrued Interest** is interest accumulated since the principal amount. **Principal amount** means the actual cash value amount of the purchase.

Credit card companies ask for a minimum amount to pay on the card each month. Let's say you purchased something for $500. The minimum amount to keep in good standing is $20.00 a month. You pay the $20.00.

The company charges an 18% APR (Annual Percentage Rate [annual means a year {12 months}]). To figure out your monthly interest take 18% ÷ 12 = 1.5%. Your purchase of $500 X 1.5% = a $7.50 charge. (Or, move the decimal point two places from the percentage symbol making it .015. 500 X .015 = $7.50.

APR: 28% is .28; high end

7.7% is .077; low end

Now, divide by 12. So, .28 ÷ 12 = .023; .077 ÷ 12 = .0064.

Next, .023 X $500 = $11.50; .0064 X 500 = $3.20—a month added to amount.

Or, .023 X $1,000 = $23; .0064 X $1,000 = $6.40.

As you can see, your purchase that you thought was a sale or deal, at the time, could end up costing you more in the long run, if you don't pay it off immediately. My rule of thumb has always been that if I can't pay it off the next month, I don't get it.

I hope you can see why credit cards exist. The credit-card company makes money off your bad spending habits. The more you spend and don't pay off your bill, the more in their pocket. Old rule: Who do you want to have the hard-earned penny, you or them?

If you don't pay the due amount each month, you become a credit risk, which means a company may charge you a higher interest rate. Or, they can decline giving you another card. However, companies are out there, who are willing to give you a card. Why? Look at the above figures. They make money off of your bad habits. As a credit risk, your FICO score plummets and the next big purchase you want to make is declined. Why? You are a risk and no good business wants to give away something for free, knowing they may never get their money back. Most businesses are in the business to make money, not to lose it. Your score tells them at a glance, if they could lose money off of you; or, whether you are a responsible person and no risk is involved.

You never want a collection agency in your life. A **Collection Agency** is hired by a company to regain their monies lost, IF you refuse to pay off the debt. They are the middle man that does whatever necessary to regain the company's product or rightful amount due. Again, your FICO score plummets if anything goes to this agency.

You do not want others to possess or to use your credit cards. A signature is required upon purchasing an item, but sadly, many merchants do not take the time to compare the transaction signature against the one written on the back of the card. One way to help with this is to make the request yourself. Or, put on the card that you want your driver's license as a means of identification.

If the card(s) are ever lost or stolen, then make a call immediately to make a report. The number is, usually, on the back of the card, so record it in your records. Check with the card company to see what their policy is on lost or stolen cards, if an illegal purchase(s) was made. Do this before you get the card to make sure you are covered. Many times, you do not have to pay for a purchase(s) you did not authorize or make.

CVV Code (or similar code): Card Verification Value code, which is a three to four digit number on the back of your credit card. It is a means to let the company know you are the holder of the card and the account is legitimate.

VISA, MasterCard, American Express, Discover Card, JCPenny, Macys, and on the list can go. Not every merchant or place of business for goods and services accept all cards. So, be wise and pick a card that you can be used and can be recognized in most places.

PAYING BILLS

Well, you've done some saving and some spending, now it is time to pay bills. You knew it would happen, sooner or later. Your hard-earned money is going to be eaten away. Don't get discouraged. Learn to be thrifty, prudent in your spending and decisions, and you will have plenty of money to enjoy.

To help you adjust to paying bills and what to expect, here is a form to help you fill in the blanks and determine what you can or cannot afford per month (see page 65):

EXAMPLE:

BILLS	PAY OUT
Apartment	$550.00
Electric\Gas	90.00
Phone	60.00
Cable\Internet	+ 100.00
TOTAL Spent	$ 800.00
As you can see this does not include @ week:	
Food	150.00
Clothes &Misc.	60.00
Gas for Car	50.00
Entertainment	60.00
Car Payment	175.00
	$ 495.00
Monthly Expenses	800.00
TOTAL Average of Expenses	$1,295.00
Car Insurance	135.00

This chart shows *an average* of expenditures. Either one of those figures can change according to your personal expenditures and companies you choose. During the month, you will have **monthly and weekly bills**. Most businesses (rental place, utilities, and cable and phone services) are monthly bills and they expect their money the **first of the month**. Some give you 7 to 10 days to pay. If not paid, you can expect a **late fee**. A late fee is a fine for not giving them their money due, *when due*. No excuses! They do not want to hear why you couldn't give them their money. After all, it is clearly documented when it is due and you should be aware of it. As a responsible person, you are expected to act responsibly and that means pay your bills. The company gave you a **service** and they deserve to get paid for what **you used**. A late fee amount can change, depending on the place of business. I can assure you, it can be hefty at times.

★ If you can't pay, then you need to let them know right away. Some businesses, however, will respect you more if you contact them <u>before it is due</u>, to let them know you ran into some difficulty. This is a time to be honest; lying will only make your situation grow worse. More often than not, they will work with you to resolve the issue. This is considered, mutual respect. Ignoring them only makes them angry and they have zero tolerance. At the same time, if this becomes a habit of not paying your bills on time, they will lose their patience and you have left a trail behind you. Result: Others will not want to work with you, either.

The rule of thumb is to have the bill money ready a week before it is due. This means you need to learn to **budget** your money, so you always have it ready to distribute it out. Before you purchase, sign a lease, or get under a contract, you should already know what you have coming in (Income: **credit** +) and expect going out (Expenses: **debit** -). In other words, what can you afford? If the Expense-debt amount of money is MORE than the Income-credit

amount, then you need to make some adjustments ★before you commit yourself to anything. Once your signature goes on a piece of paper, it is legal and binding. Use the chart to help you determine this.

BUDGET

Budget: It is an overall look at what your take-home pay (credit + [Income]) and a fair estimation cost of what bills will be paid that month (debt - [Expenses]). Included in this, to help you better prepare a list, would be an amount determined by your past experience and spending habits. For past spending habits, don't use a conservative amount to determine your budget; use an amount, at least, $50 - $100 above. This gives you room, if something unexpected arrives. This can only help you, not hurt you, because any amount above you didn't spend is a savings, money in your pocket. In other words, if you spend $25 a week on fast-food drinks and hamburgers, than use that amount under food, or pleasure. If you regularly go shopping and spend around $50 a week, than add that into the budgeting figures. These figures can be debits, but end up being credits, if you don't spend the money—so a savings.

Budgeting helps you to always be aware and to stay afloat, even if tough times come.

Remember, when you budget, some bills are consistently the same each month (rent, car pymt., insurance, etc.) and some fluctuate with usage (utilities, phone, food, entertainment, etc. [so use an average or higher figure]). Consider adding into your budget something you might be planning for in the near future, like a car and the added expenses included with it: Insurance, gas, maintenance, etc.

For this example, your monthly take-home pay is $1,500.

BUDGET $1,500 Month

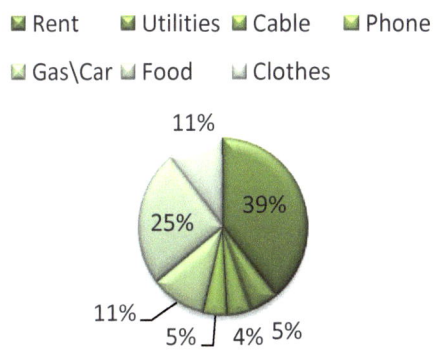

■ Rent   ■ Utilities ■ Cable   ■ Phone
■ Gas\Car ■ Food   ■ Clothes

11%

39%

25%

11%

5% 4% 5%

CREDIT (+)	DEBIT (-)	
$1,500		
	Rent	$ 550
	Utilities	75
	Cable	65
	Phone	65
	Gas\Car	150
	Food	350
	+Clothes	150
$1,500		
Savings: **$95**		$1,405

As you can see from the Examples, at a glance, you *know* what your monthly budget will be, **before** you start spending. If you do this, you will never go into **debt**.

Remember this always, concerning debt, never budget above your take-home pay, to live above and beyond your means to pay off

any outstanding debts. EX: Using the chart, you have a $95 savings for the month. If you put yourself in a $300 debt, it will take you, at least, three months to get out of the debt (3 X $95 = $285). During those three months, unexpected spending can occur: birthdays, gift giving, dinner dates, fines, car repair, etc. Each time you accumulate a debt, it is added on top of the amount already in place. If you didn't have the $300 in May, what makes you think you will have it in June, July, August, etc.? With the inability to pay, the debt mounts until you become stressed and worried. This takes a toll and your health can be affected. Staying within your income, at all times, gives you a care-free lifestyle, as far as money is concerned. ★You cannot pay out what you do not have coming in. ★ Another job, overtime, selling what you have are the only options (legally) you may have, in order to resolve your dilemma. Getting a loan isn't always the best means, because it is another item to tag onto your budget. Also, if you used a credit card, you are accumulating compound interest on the $300.

Knowing your budget helps you make sound decisions, if you decide to purchase anything of substantial value. Let's say a car. By looking at your budget, you will know an amount you can afford or not afford, when it comes to the monthly amount due for a car. If you have a savings of $250 each month, than you know you have, at least, $100 to put towards a car each month. **Never** use the exact amount saved; use an amount, at least, $50-$100 below. Don't forget, with a car, you have insurance, title, deed, taxes, gas, maintenance, and expenditures.

★Know everything, before you make a sound transaction. ★ Look at the Debt-Credit ratio. Simply put, what can you afford? Consider how many years you will have to be responsible for the debt as well. These days, it can be four to five years, depending on the loan. Try to imagine where you will be in four to five years. Is the debt of the car worth it, at this time? If you waited, you might be able to afford the bells-and-whistle car in the future. Now, you may have to use the public transportation or an old reliable clunker. Don't buy by the look of the car; buy by what is in your ability to pay. The bells-and-whistle car can come later. You might even enjoy it later, because you didn't have stress over the first car every day. No regrets, so you can have an enjoyable and satisfying experience with your new purchase.

It can, also, be beneficial to have a month's worth of money in reserve, sitting in the savings that equals your monthly bills. It stays in your reserve, which means, it is there, but you never touch it. As you get older, it becomes prudent to accumulate enough money to pay off six month's worth of bills or up to a year. This way, you have room to move and breath, in case of an emergency. And, emergencies do happen. So, if the expenses are $1,400 a month, you should have, at least, $1,400 above your savings or $9,000 accumulated for six months to pay off debts, in case of trouble.

Let's look at the chart (page 39):

Rent, Utilities, Phone, Car Payment, and Cable, more often than not, are NEVER changed. You can expect this amount every month for at least a year. So, these will never be a surprise.

Food, Clothes, miscellaneous, gas, and entertainment, these can all be altered to fit what is in your pocketbook\wallet. Rule of thumb to stay out of debt is: YOU DON'T HAVE IT, THAN DON'T SPEND IT. No matter how tempting it can be, don't spend what you do not have. This comes under the NEED or WANT category. Always ask yourself this: "Do I NEED this and without it NOW, I can't get by or survive? Or, is it something I WANT and if I wait, it will be available another day when the money is in my pocket?" Don't let a sale trick you into buying. Sales are always around, if not in one store, than in another.

Car Insurance, usually, doesn't change, but it can be a monthly or a one-time, six-month payment. This amount ranges with your driving record: your age, accidents, tickets, bad driving habits, etc. and the make of car, year of car, rating of the car (safety issues). So, before you buy a car, you might want to do some research and see how the insurance companies feel about the Make, Model, and Track record of the vehicle and you. Always do your research and get the best deal for you. Expect anywhere from $450 to over a thousand every six months (much higher if a new driver). Or, $75 to over $167 a month.

(Important Note: Today, many companies are, now, requiring that ONLY the owner of the vehicle has coverage, not any driver. If someone drives your vehicle, with permission or not, and they wreck, you may not be covered for the accident. It could be all out-of-pocket expenses.)

Inside the Insurance quote:

BI-Bodily Injury **Liability** (means you are responsible): It covers other people, if they are hurt involving your car, this covers their injuries or death. This is good to have, if they pursue a lawsuit against you. Does not cover you.

PD-Property Damage: Covers you if your car causes property damage, which can mean their car, actual damage to a property, a home, etc. This is good to have, if they pursue a lawsuit against you.

Comprehensive Coverage: Covers your vehicle, and others, for losses that result from an incident other than a collision. EX: If stolen, damage by flood, fire, or an animal. It agrees to pay for the damages.

Collision: Covers damage to your car when your vehicle hits, or is hit by, another vehicle or object. It pays to fix your car.

Underinsured Motorist Bodily Injury: If someone has insufficient coverage, this pays the insured members of your household and passengers for damages, injuries, or death caused by their negligence.

PID-Personal Injury Protection: Covers the medical, hospital, and funeral expenses of the insured and others in their vehicle and pedestrians struck by him.

Deductible: This is what you pay out of pocket, if you activate any of these coverages. If the accident came to $20,000 and your policy states a $2,500 deductible, you pay out of pocket the $2,500. The insurance covers the rest.

Companies offer more coverage than listed or some are not in all states. Check what is best for you and what deductible is comfortable for you.

Check the insurance to make sure ALL driver's of YOUR vehicle are covered under your plan.

Rent: Is a set amount each month. This amount can vary as you do research in your area on what apartment to choose. Expensive doesn't mean the best for you. A one-bedroom apartment for $1,100 and one for $450 is, still, a one-bedroom apartment. Each has a kitchen, bathroom, and living area. The differences in price are the amenities: the area\location, club house, the look\appearance, washer\dryer, size, etc.

Also, rent means you are being allowed to use *their* property and possessions for a period of time. Nothing in the apartment belongs to you. It is theirs and they expect it to be left the way they presented it to you: working and in reasonable condition.

Utilities (Gas\Electric\Trash\Water): The amount fluctuates. What you owe can depend upon the season. Winter requires more heat and Summer more air conditioning, so the bill can be higher than Spring and Fall. Check with the utility company or the rental department and they can tell you what the previous owners paid.

This gives you a year's worth of information to determine if you can fit the amount of the bill into your budget. Use the higher figure to determine your budget, or average over 12 months.

<u>Cable</u> (Internet, Phone, WIFI): More times than not, an area can have one or two main companies to choose from. Again, get what you can afford, not want. This amount can vary from $40 conservative to over $150 a month. As you start out, the bells and whistles package may have to wait. Consider that a movie package may cost $40 a month, while going out to the movies may cost you $20 to $80 a month. So, which might be better for you: going out to the movies or staying home and watching them?

<u>Groceries</u>: Budgeting when you buy groceries fluctuates each day, week, and month. This method I am about to explain may seem odd, but more times than not, it does work. Use an *average* to get the amount of the cost of the food you purchase, before you approach the register. Here is how: Each item, no matter the cost, it becomes $3.50. By time you get to the register, you will have a figure that will be close to what the actual bill will be. So, if you bought 15 items, your bill will be around $53 ($3.50 X 15 = $52.50). It might be slightly above or below, but you can count on it being around $50. Or, at home, when you are making out your grocery list, you can see at a glance *approximately* how much your groceries will be. In my own life, I have always been within five dollars of the actual amount. (Or, smart ones, take a calculator.)

Buy one and get one free might be a good option to consider when buying groceries on a limited budget. You can stock up quickly by taking advantage of these options. Just make sure they are items you will eat. Check the local ads to see what is in season and on sale. Use coupons and these can, also, be found online.

Personal Note: I don't advocate debt of any kind. There is nothing more rewarding than to own everything you have. The only two items that may be considered as given debts for the average household would be a home and a car. The cost of these can be above the average person's ability to save enough to pay them off outright. I didn't say this was impossible; I said it is not likely for the average person.

Rule of thumb: Don't purchase anything unless you know it can be paid off within a month, or a reasonable amount of time. ★ Again, adding debt to debt is never wise. ★ Purchasing one item at a time and paying for it outright is far better than accumulating a room full of things that you don't own outright. No one can ever take what you own away; **you own it**.

With your first place, the necessary items to purchase would be a bed and chair. Other things can wait. Never overlook garage sales in nice areas, thrift stores, Goodwill, and the like. It pays to look at all your options before making a purchase. A furniture "sale" doesn't always mean you are getting a deal. They have sales on unsellable items to get you in the store, while many stores use this to mark up the rest, the more desirable and appealing pieces. Be aware. Shop around, compare, and, at times, negotiate the end price. You never know; they might negotiate a deal. After all, would you like the penny in your pocket or their pocket? Even pennies can add up.

Consider this as well, or at least in the future: Rent or Own. To me, renting has always been a means of throwing money down the toilet (so to speak). Owning a home, if you can afford the payments, is an investment. Yes; even in today's economy, if you buy right and do your research, a home can benefit you in the long run. If an apartment cost you $500 a month and buying a home costs you $450; it might be to your benefit to get the home. However! Other costs come with owning a home: taxes, insurance, higher utility bills,

maintenance, etc. Look at your budget. Weigh all pros and cons. More importantly, ask your parents for advice. They have been there and done that; they know.

You can decide how long you will make monthly payments: 15, 20, 25, or 30 years. Obviously, the more years you choose, the less the monthly amount. But, it takes more years to pay off. Included in the payment is the **principal**, or amount credited to actual cost of home. **Interest** is the amount that goes to financial institution for lending you the money: one part to home, other to lender. Ex: $280 is principal and $200 is interest, which equals $480 monthly-house payment. you can always add more money to put on the principal, which lowers the actual-home loan.

At the closing for a home, you must come up with thousands of dollars to make the deal. Rule of thumb, as with an apartment, take a third (or up to 35% [statistics say as high as 45%, which I believe can make it more difficult to stay afloat and be comfortable]) of your income away and that can be an average figure of what your monthly payment maybe; can you afford this? If you can't make it with a third of your income gone, then it isn't wise to go forward.

Rent or House Payment with $1,500 monthly, take-home pay:

$1,500 X .35 = $525 or $1,500 X .45 = $675, which leaves $975 or $825 left for expenses. This is why *I believe* it is more feasible to make ends meet by remaining to the 30% ($500 payment & $1,000 left for expenses), because you know the home you buy will have to stay around $500 a month (less risk).

Okay, it is time to put this into perspective.

Let's say you make $8 an hour and you work 40 hours a week. $8 X 8 = $64 a day. $64 X 5 (days you worked) = $320 ÷ 3 = $214 (take home pay for week [remember, the third goes to taxes])

$214 x 4 = **$856 a month**.

EXAMPLE:

BILLS	PAY OUT
Apartment	$550.00
Electric\Gas	90.00
Phone	60.00
Cable\Internet	+ 100.00
TOTAL Spent	$ 800.00

As you can see this does not include @ week:

Food	150.00
Clothes &Misc.	60.00
Gas for Car	50.00
Entertainment	60.00
Car Payment	175.00
	$ 495.00
Monthly Expenses	800.00
TOTAL Average of Expenses	$1,295.00
Car Insurance	135.00
Take Home pay a month ($8 an hour 40 hrs. a week)	856.00
Take Home pay a month ($10 an hour 40 hrs. a week)	$1,066.67
Take Home Pay a month ($12 an hour 40 hrs. a week)	$1,280.00

You brought in $856 (Credit +) and spent $800 (Debit -). As you can see from the chart, you have $56 left to spend for the whole month or $14 for the week. And all you did was pay the necessary bills. You needed almost $500 more to live comfortably. This is reality. So, do you get discouraged or get wise?

Things like the food, clothes, gas, and entertainment can range from $50 to $320 a week to fudge and recalculate. However, to budget wisely, you must always keep them in the back of your mind, because these do occur. This is where you can learn to save and put aside for another time. Do you *need* that pizza for Friday night or that new shirt on sale this week, or can they wait for another time?

▶▶ What does all this mean? It means that when you apply for a job, you KNOW what income you **need** to be on your own. ◀◀ Before you look for work, sit and calculate the amount you will **need** per hour to live a comfortable existence on your own. The minimum

wage for today can range from $5.00 to $7.25 an hour, depending on where you live. So, that can mean from $200 - $290 for 40 hours of work a week. Or, $133 - $193 take-home pay *average*. So, $532 - $772 a month to budget and know where you stand.

Living alone? You might consider a roommate. Getting the friend that always borrowed and never gave anything back wouldn't be the first choice. Look for someone who is responsible and takes things seriously enough that they are considerate, thoughtful, dependable, reliable, not a leech, but someone you can trust and believe to do their part. If you want to know if living with them might be a consideration, than look at their bedroom and living space. If you think any of that will change, think again. However, if you were a slob, too, then living together after a while might get pretty disgusting. It isn't one mess now; it is two. Mom won't be there to clean up after you. It is, now, a matter of what are you willing to tolerate?

★When signing a lease, make sure both names are on the lease. If one walks out and your name is the only one on it, YOU are the responsible party, not them. If they destroy something, YOU are the responsible party to pay the damages. Your only recourse to get back what you feel they owe you is in court, small claims. Just make sure you have plenty of pictures, something in writing with their signature that can prove your story. As far as the court is concerned that is all it will be is a story, unless you have <u>solid documentation</u> that they were suppose to pay rent and they would pay damages if something occurred. A she said-he said does not work in the court, rarely. When it comes to someone's money, the friend relationship takes a back seat, even if they were a childhood friend you grew up with. It is survival time, so make sure you have a contract with their signature and it is all spelled out with the details: Dates, name, agreement, amount of money, etc.

Rule of thumb: People who are known to take advantage will keep doing it until they are stopped. They are the Takers and not Givers.

Your record of paying your bills on time and being responsible DOES follow you into life. Known as a **FICO** (Fair Isaac Corporation) score ranging from 300 and 850, a measure of **credit**. Obviously, the higher the score, the better you look on paper.

Any organization where a money transaction takes place, involving you, they look at the FICO score. If your score is high, they know you will pay on time your debts of responsibility. This is the guide many use to determine, if they can TRUST you or not. They don't want to hear your sob story of how someone took advantage of you and put you in the bad light. All they are going to do is question why you didn't stop them, before they ran your good reputation into the ground. Some Organizations that use the FICO: a credit-card company, auto dealership, bank, Rental company, utility companies, anything involving a form of loan or purchase with intent to pay later, etc.

AN APARTMENT
or
HOME

So, it's your first place away from home, or first apartment you rent. You are, now, or will soon be, a **tenant**, or, eventually a **homeowner**. What can you expect or know what to look for, as you decide where to live?

Back to your budget—Know what you can afford. Typically, as with buying a home, you can afford something that is a third (as high as 35%) of your take-home pay for the month. So, if that is $1,500, you can afford a home or apartment and stay reasonably comfortable with the payments and living expenses, at $500. Don't forget, you have to anticipate all the other expenses and you don't want to drain your income and leave no room for a breather. With $2,100 income, expect around $700 affordable-rent payment; $3,500 income around $1,100.

Don't go by outside appearances. Know your environment. It's best to go back to it several times during different times of the day. Weekends are best, because most people aren't at work. Look for: heavy traffic, a busy street, a barking dog, nosey neighbors, upkeep, trash laying around, loud music, someone who fixes cars or motorcycles and revs them all hours of the day, observe how others maintain their possessions, which will give you a relatively good idea on how they will be with your possessions. In other words, if they don't take care of their stuff, they are not going to care about yours. Generally speaking, this is true. Outside of this rule, when you see a home or apartment unkempt, could it be the elderly who can't, single mothers who can't and are barely getting by, or the disabled.

Go help them; be a good neighbor to them. Just be aware of what you are getting yourself into, because this is a year's lease.

What's the view from your apartment window or balcony? Is it something you can live with for at least a year? Does the apartment stink, because of tobacco smoke, water, or pet damage?

Look at the surroundings and see if it is a safe neighborhood\area. The police are the best ones to ask, because they know the area. They can tell you the problems they have with the residence. Again, get online and check out certain sites that can give you some idea on what to expect, like for pedophiles.

Bars on all the windows might be your first indicator that not all is well in that part of town. Beware and wonder, "Why are they there?"

If you like riding a bike, running early in the morning, or taking walks, will this be an area that can give you what you want? Does it seem safe? Does it have good lighting around the building at night for safety? Is it patrolled by their security guard?

The schemers and takers are out there and all you are to them is fresh meat. Just know that not everyone is looking out for you. So, it is important to have a keen ear and eyes to see what they are not divulging.

Check the building's past history for roaches, plumbing problems (leaks and sinks being stopped up), and flea problems in carpet because of past pets. Check all appliances to make sure they work: dishwasher, garbage disposal, stove, oven (look inside for burned on grease and smells), refrigerator (check for smells and mold), fans, toilet flushing, and light switches. Take a minute and run the water in the sinks and bathtub. If you get an odd smell, noise, or discolored water, you have the opportunity to ask why it is in that condition.

If they have a pool, then make sure it is maintained and the chlorine is keeping the pool clean and sparkly.

Stand in the middle of the apartment and listen to see if you can hear what your neighbors are doing on the other side of the wall. This is vitally important in the bedroom. You want to get a good-night's sleep, than you better make sure the neighbor wants that as well. So, listen.

Ask if they have a maintenance man on hand, or do they hire out the work. This just helps you to know whether you will get help quickly, if something goes wrong, or will it be slow.

Check for cable and internet hookups and the options for that area. Note where the outlets are and are these convenient?

Try to imagine you in the living space. Do you like it and can all your stuff fit? Do they have enough storage? Make sure the washer and dryer facility isn't far from you to walk, while trying to carry a load of laundry, and make sure it is a 24\7, or has convenient hours. Does it have good lighting, security cameras, and are they all working properly?

A good apartment is always freshly painted and the carpets and floors clean, before you move into it. This is an expected service. If they are not, then it gives you a heads up on what to expect from them for the year—not much. The old saying, "You get what you pay for," might ring true in this case.

Note the parking area. Is it far or close? Does it have room for two cars or extra space when company comes? Most apartments have a designated space for your car, so don't feel like you can take another's spot, just because their car isn't parked in it.

Are pets allowed and can you live with that from other neighbors, especially a habitual, barking dog nearby?

Note the cost of everything: Amount of rent per month, cable, utilities, phone, trash, use of club or for parties, etc. Be aware that most apartments require a month's rent in advance, plus another fee to hold, if damages occur while you rented the apartment. So, let's say it is $500 a month. You may need $500 + $500 = $1,000. Note:

the money will be returned once the lease is up and the apartment is okayed that no damage was done. Expect the utilities companies to get a **deposit** (only once) from you, too, when you make the initial contract. This is money above the bill amount and each company is different, so ask.

Picking a roommate: I discussed this a bit earlier, but this is important to add some more thoughts to help you make a wise decision. If you get a roommate, do you mind them sitting naked on your new couch and throwing a greasy pizza box on the cushion? Do you mind someone tipping their beer onto your precious coffee table that your Grandmother gave you as a gift?

Will you always be the one cleaning up after everyone, or will they help?

Will they have people in and out of the apartment all hours? If so, can you live with that? Are you going to have an arrangement that when they have "special" company over, you need to leave? Before long, you have taken up residence in the nearby coffee-shop all night, because they are always *busy* with company?

Do they always borrow and never return anything? Remember; this is money out of your pocket, hard-earned money.

Okay, you got the picture.

▶▶A **lease** is a binding contract by law. READ the contract before you sign! ◀◀ Once your signature goes on any paper, money is exchanged, then it is a mutual understanding, both parties in agreement with like minds and expectances.

You are *using* their property for a period of time; you agreed to this. You agreed to leave it in the best condition possible, as you found it when you rented it. So, putting a fist through a door; yes; you just bought the door. A hole in the wall, yes; you just paid for the repairs for them to fix it. Carpet stained through carless spills, yes; you just bought new carpet or a carpet cleaner to clean up the

damage. You did the damage; you pay. It is that simple. Leasing does not mean you own anything in that apartment. Everything stays where it was put.

With <u>purchasing a home</u>, many of my suggestions apply. Look at purchase price from original\built. Has it increased or declined; ask why? Look at the area, upkeep (paint, windows, mailbox, things around the garage and sides, window treatments [curtains or sheets, torn blinds, broken windows, and screens]) of the homes around yours, including landscaping and lawn, especially back yards, pets, and smells. These are indicators of the other owners around you. Again, pay attention to street lights, sidewalks, the street full of parked cars, etc. Decide what you will tolerate or be exasperated with. These, also, can bring down or up the value of your home.

Inside the home, ask vital questions and get proof of their answers, including cost of utility bills and property tax for 12 months. Know the purchase dates of the roof, electric, furnace, air conditioning, softener, refrigerator, stove, etc. Reason is simple. If they are old, you can count on having to redo or purchase them very soon, which means an expensive mistake, later. It might be wise to get home insurance that covers a new-home purchase for such items.

Don't just ask, look at each item (pipes, fixtures, electric wiring, cracks in walls, water damage, etc.), up close. Pay attention to water damage, if any, around home: floor, woodwork, rust, mold, corrosion, etc. Look closely at roof, attic, crawl space, brick or outside-home treatment, soffits and gutters, etc. Do not rely on just the **inspector**, who is sent by financial institution to make sure home has value to purchase-price ratio (in other words, is it worth their money to lend to you, in case you cannot make payments?).

Foreclosure: Lender, money institution, takes back the home, because you did not keep up monthly obligation.

CAR

Purchasing a car: Well, obviously, you need to know what you want first, before you can make a sound decision. Again, look at your budget. A good car can range from $4,500 to $7,000 or $10,000. A brand new car can range from $10,000 to $35,000 (or more). Unless you had the money outright and can pay in cash, you will need a **loan**.

As an example of a loan: A $5,000 car with a loan for four years, at 7.5% interest, your payment will be $121.41 a month. Total paid is $5,875.47.

$10,000, four years, 7.5% = $244.81 a month, total=$11,750.95.

$22,000, five years, 7.5% = $446.35 a month, total=$26,780.72.

This doesn't include taxes, title, or insurance.

An interest rate varies, so check around. They can be from 3.80% to 7%, give or take.

A loan: an amount of money needed to make a purchase. An organization, bank (the **Lender**), agrees to give you (the **Borrower**) a loan.

Being a first-time buyer, you might need what is called a **Co-signer:** a parent, relative, or rich friend. A Co-signer is someone who agrees to pay, if you don't pay. They are not the responsible party to pay the loan; they DO NOT pay the monthly bill; you do. They are like a safety net and agree to *help you* stand on your feet alone. Just remember, if you default on the loan, they are responsible. And, they can sue for damages to recoup their losses.

Default simply means you did not abide by the legal obligations to pay and so, they (dealership) have a right to gain back

possession of the vehicle—**repossession**. This doesn't mean you are out of the woods, yet. You, still, have the loan. If you took a loan out for $3,000 and the car can be sold for $1,500 and all you paid was $500, you, still, owe the outstanding balance: $1,000. A good Co-signer, however, might step in before it gets that far. Remember: this isn't the kind of bad business that you want to start your life out with. You want it clean and upright.

Most dealerships can provide an option for a loan or you can research this on your own and find the best deal. **A loan** is a transaction where the Financial Institution lends you the amount of money *needed* to complete the transaction. Let's say, $3,000. They, usually, don't agree to loan out that amount of money without some form of **collateral**. Collateral is something that is equal or above the amount requested. In this instance, it could be the car. But, if they feel the car is only worth $2,500, you, more than likely, won't see the $3,000. They want something of equal value in case you can't pay. This can be your savings, bonds, home, anything of equal or more value. Your ten-speed bike isn't going to work here.

Okay, loan is approved. You are, now, the **Debtor**. A debtor has a debt and is responsible to pay it off.

The Financial Institution (the **Lender**) handed over $3,000 and you own the car. Congrats! Well, that was short lived, because you don't really *own* the car; the Financial Institution owns the car until the debt is paid. Well, it felt good while it lasted. Oh, cheer up. You do have your first car and, no matter what, it feels good. So, enjoy. With a debt, you don't have the title to the car; the loan company keeps it until the loan is paid. A **lien** (a debt owed) is on the title. Once the debt is paid, you are given the original copy of the title. You, now, own the car outright.

So, now, we deal with **interest**. Interest is what you agreed to give the Financial Institution for using their money. Let's say you took the loan out for four years. Depending on the interest, you would have paid $3,652 at the end of the four years (I am purely speculating. It could be more or less, depending on the rate of interest.)

At 10% for four years (48 months), your payment, per month, can be $76.09. So, it cost you an extra $652 to buy the car. The Financial Institution will give you a payment book and schedule, with amount owed and date due for the payment. So, each month, you tear out the slip and send in your payment (check) with the right amount. Let me add: At any time, you can pay off the loan faster. You can do this by doubling up the payments. Or, instead of $76.09, you make the check out for $100. $23.91 will be subtracted from the **principal**. Principal is the original amount given: $3,000.

Being responsible and paying this debt is a good opportunity to build your FICO score.

Deciding upon a car: Pride aside, I am not the best one to give advice on this. I do know enough, however, to help you a bit. A car to me has always been five wheels and an engine. Four tires, one steering wheel, and the whole thing better get me from point A to point B. If it does that much, I am happy.

Never purchase a car without doing the research on it first. You can do this through the **VIN** #, which has 17 characters. The VIN, or Vehicle Identification Number, gives the history of the car. This can tell you if it has ever been in a major accident or repairs.

Depending on Make and Model, you can find the VIN #:
- On the door frame/door post of the front doors (usually driver's but sometimes passenger's)
- On the dash near the windshield
- On the engine itself (machined pad on front of engine)
- On the car's firewall
- In the left-hand inner wheel arch

- On the steering wheel/steering column
- On the radiator support bracket
- On your car's title, registration, guarantee/maintenance book or on the declarations page of your auto insurance policy

Don't skip this step. Next, you can look up the car in the **Kelley Blue Book**. This gives you how much your new car is really worth. If the Dealer is asking $3,000 and you find the value is $1,500, then you better find out why the discrepancy.

Well, I did my part. The best advice I can give from here would bring a reliable mechanic to check out the car before you buy it. He can check to see if it is running well, the tires don't need replaced, or major engine issues won't exist. These can be more money out of your pocket.

This happened to me, so I might as well share this experience. I found a car that was, to me, a dream car. The Dealer seemed anxious to sell it to me. I didn't see one thing wrong with it and they assured me it was in great condition. The price didn't fit the car. It seemed too low. I almost bought it, but I took my own advice and asked a mechanic. He laughed. The reason wasn't the car. He said it was a dream car. The problem: if it ever broke down, all the parts were foreign. The costs for repairs would be astronomical. Anything it needed would have to be shipped into the states. Few shops would know how to repair it. Lesson learned: Buyer Beware!

Insurance: All companies are different in each state. Check to see their requirements. The bottom line is this: if you damage another person's car or they get injured, you are responsible. You must pay or they can sue you and get their due monies through the court system. Insurance gets you out of this mess. Roughly, the insurance can cost between $750 (average) to well over a thousand dollars a year for the specific coverage you want. This is one area you don't want to skip. Some states, if not all, require it by law.

Registration\Title\Tags: Find the Courthouse closes to you and call to make sure what you need. Here is a list for you to bring along: Proof of ownership, insurance, proof of identity (Driver's License, Birth Certificate), payment for sales taxes and fees, information on the loan company, purchase price of vehicle, type of vehicle, Odometer reading, which can be found behind the steering wheel.

Side notes: This is your vehicle. It isn't a toy; it can be a killing machine. I don't want to get dramatic, but you need to take this seriously. When you pull onto any road, this is not a race car and the road the Indy 500. It is a public domain and ▶▶lives are in your hands◀◀. Your eyes should be looking in a 360° radius. You should be aware of everything around you <u>at all times</u>: sides, behind, in front, below, and way out in all directions, especially in a neighborhood, you need to look toward the yards and sidewalks. A child chasing a ball, a dog or cat running, a biker losing their balance, a person pulling out from their driveway, they all might not see you. See them!

Use the rearview mirror often. It can be a lifesaver. Someone who is speeding, closing in behind you, and can't stop in time, you used the mirror. It could give you the life-saving edge to get out of the way.

At 60 miles an hour, it takes at least six car lengths for you to stop safely. 30 mph, it takes three car lengths. Riding a bumper won't get you to your destination any faster. Sit back, relax, and enjoy the ride.

Do we even have to say this? Drinking, drugs and a car in motion don't mix. I had a relative cause an accident that took another's life. His life, forty years later, has never been the same. Texting and using a cell phone irresponsibly can kill, or damage a life permanently—a life sentence that you imposed upon them

thoughtlessly and carelessly. Plain talk is what is needed to make this clear. Is any of this worth another's life? Once it happens, your nightmare just began, too. The emotional and financial scars can last a long time.

Letting someone use your car. You are responsible, even if they did the careless act of causing damage, whether to the car, the other car, or person(s). You can get sued if damages are caused by them. That quick trip to the store that they promised would be okay, can mean years of anguish for you, because they used your car irresponsibly, especially if they drank or were high. This is your property and with that comes accountability. Think wisely and use good judgment.

The car: The tires need the right **psi** (pounds per square inch) and this can be seen on the side of the tire. In other words, make sure the tire has good air pressure or you can run into serious problem: wearing the tire prematurely, causing you to use more fuel, or not having a firmer grip on the road. Make sure the tire isn't going bald or wearing unevenly on the sides.

Oil: On average, every three months or 3,000 miles have the oil changed. On the dash, you can usually see the miles you drove from the last oil change. Check for the best deals and a reputable business.

Battery and Maintenance: Make sure you have your car checked, at least, once or twice a year to make sure it is running at optimal performance. The better you take care of your car, the longer it will last and less expense out of pocket.

Gas: Make sure you fill it up with the right gas for the make and model of the car: leaded, diesel, regular, high octane. The price of a fill up can be as much as $50 or more. In general, depending on the car, you can go 30 miles per gallon of gas. So, if the full tank is 10 gallons, you can go approx. 300 miles, before you run out of gas.

Lights: make sure all lights are working, not broken, and clean from debris. You can get a ticket or warning, if lights have a problem.

Clean Car in and Out: Items floating around on the inside of the vehicle can cause an accident. A loose bottle or rolling item can go under the brake or accelerator, causing you to lose control of the car. A sudden stop can cause an object to become a projectile, causing injury or damage. The outside needs a good washing to keep all windows clear for a safe view. It, also, helps to prolong the covering of the car to keep from premature rust and damage. Your car reflects you.

READ THE CAR'S MANUAL.

FOOD SHOPPING

This is personal preference, so I won't linger on this subject too long. However, to make sure your kitchen runs smoothly, I have a few helpful suggestions on what to stock in the kitchen. These items and foods can be a good start in the pantry.

Basics:

- A good fry pan and medium size pot
- Coffee Pot
- Large stirring spoon, spatula, and meat fork
- Plates, bowls, and silverware
- Cups for coffee and drinks
- A casserole dish
- Can opener
- Baking sheet
- Measuring Spoons & Cups

This isn't much and I left out a few things, because over time, they will accumulate in your kitchen anyway.

Food in the Cupboard

Again, personal preference, but if you have these few items, you can cook just about anything.

- Flour
- Sugar
- Salt & Pepper
- Baking Powder & Baking Soda
- Cooking Oil (Peanut, Olive)

- Yeast (Packaged)
- Tomato Sauce
- Butter
- Vanilla Extract
- Frozen Juices
- Tea & Coffee
- Jar of minced garlic
- Onions (bag of frozen if you don't cook often)
- Potatoes
- A variety of noodles (spaghetti, macaroni, egg)
- Eggs
- Italian Seasonings, All-purpose seasoning
- Keep 1 lb. packages of ground chuck in the freezer
- Canned kidney beans
- Spicy seasonings
- Bisquick Mix
- Raisins
- Chocolate chips
- Coco Powder
- Bread and rolls
- Peanut Butter & Jelly
- Frozen Vegetables
- Canned Soups: Cream of Anything (celery-mushroom), Cheese, Chicken, and Tomato
- Popcorn

This list can go on forever. With these few items, you can make chili, spaghetti, pancakes, muffins, rolls, pizza, cookies, cake, baked, fried, and mashed potatoes, a good breakfast, lunch, or dinner. Yum.

Get your mom's favorite recipes and make your own Cookbook. Cooking is nothing more than following the formula exactly and you can never go wrong.

When grocery shopping, it is wise to eat before you go. Going in the store hungry, typically, will cause you to purchase more than you anticipated. Items around the counter are there for a reason, so you buy something that you didn't plan. Buy as much frozen items as possible, they last longer and are always on hand and don't spoil. Frozen items, however, last only so long in the fridge, before they get freezer burn. Buy foods in season. Cheap items are typically put on the high and low shelves and the more popular-expensive brands are at eye level.

A **stove**, you cook on top of it with pots and pans. An **oven**, you put baking sheets and casserole dishes into it. A **microwave** oven (which I never liked so don't use), you throw something in and it cooks fast (never put metal inside!). A **toaster oven** (a must if single or for two) to bake small items and toast bread. It doesn't take up much space; it doesn't heat up the home like a big oven, which makes it most economical. Just make sure that the cooking dishes you buy will fit into it. Downsize the recipes to fit into it, too.

Well, that about covers it. I hope this book is a help and can get you started on your life with very few speed bumps.

I wish you all well, with a life filled with peace, love, and happiness. Enjoy the adventure.

Bye for now!

BUDGET FORM

BILLS	PAY OUT
Apartment	$_____
Electric\Gas	_____
Phone	_____
Cable\Internet	_____
TOTAL Spent	_____

As you can see this does not
include expenses for the week:

Food	_____
Clothes &Misc.	_____
Gas for Car	_____
Entertainment	_____
Car Payment	_____

Monthly Expenses	_____
TOTAL Average of Expenses	
Car Insurance	_____

Take Home Pay a month:
($_____ an hour 40 hrs. a
week)=_____

How to do a Pie Graph

In order to see your expenses at a glance and the percentage, I am adding the formula from the graph. It doesn't take long to do this, once you get the hang of it. Use the figures from Page 36:

Step 1:

Rent	$ 550.00
Electric\Gas	90.00
Phone	60.00
Cable	100.00
TOTAL	$ 800.00

Step 2: To do the formula, know that a circle is 360°

Formula: $\dfrac{Total\ of\ Each\ Item}{Total\ of\ ALL\ Items} = \dfrac{X}{360°}$

$\dfrac{550}{800} = \dfrac{X}{360°}$ 360 x 550 = 198,000 ÷ 800 = 247°

$\dfrac{90}{800} = \dfrac{X}{360°}$ 360 x 90 = 32,400 ÷ 800 =   41°

$\dfrac{60}{800} = \dfrac{X}{360°}$ 360 x 60 = 21,600 ÷ 800 =   27°

$\dfrac{100}{800} = \dfrac{X}{360°}$ 360 x 100 = 36,000 ÷ 800 =   45°

                                  + _____

                           Total   360°

Step 3: You add all the results and the total should come to 360°.

Step 4: Mark off a circle with lines—half point across is 180°- line across; above and below the line mark the 90° ⊕ and 45° ⊕ angles. From there, you use the separate degrees to mark within the circle. In this case: 247° (Apart.), 41° (Electric), 27° (Phone), and 45° (Cable).

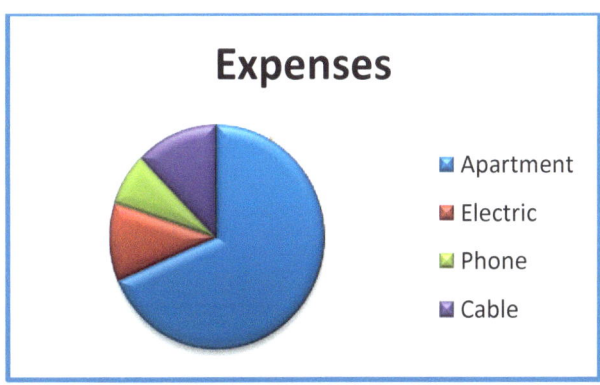

Method 2

Another way is to get a percentage of your expenses.
EX with Formula:

$$\frac{Expense}{Take\ Home\ Pay} = \frac{X}{100}$$

Using the figures from Page 37 and Income at $1,500:

$\frac{550}{1500} = \frac{X}{100}$ 550 x 100 = 55,000 ÷ 1,500 = 36.66 or 37%

$\frac{90}{1500} = \frac{X}{100}$ 90 x 100 = 9,000 ÷ 1,500 = 6.00 or 6%

$\frac{175}{1500} = \frac{X}{100}$ 175 x 100 = 17,500 ÷ 1,500 = 11.66 or 12%

ETC. . . .

Electric ($90) 6%; Phone ($60) 4%; Cable ($100) 7%; Food ($150)
10%; Clothes ($60) 4%; Gas ($50) 3%; Entertainment ($60) 4%; Car
($175) 12%; Savings ($205) 14%
The percentage should equal 100 or 100%

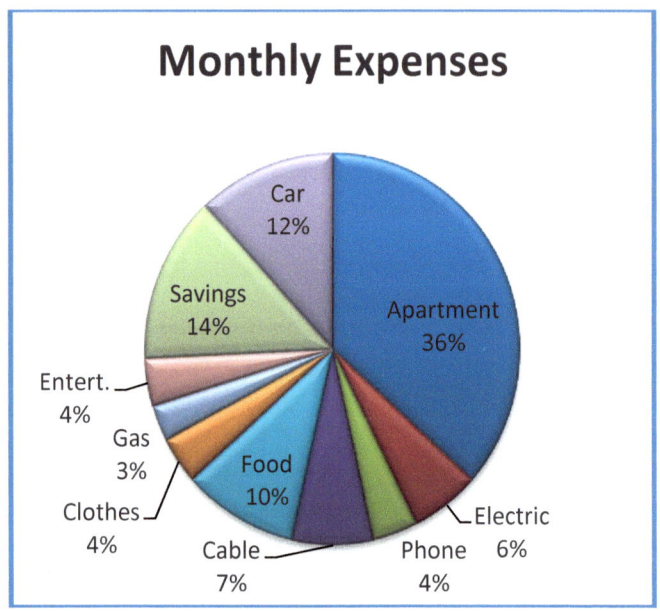

As you can see, at a glance, you know where the bulk of your
income is being used up. Some items are fixed, so you cannot change
them to help in your budget. Many of the others, you have control
over them, which allows you to save or spend accordingly.

I know some of these figures seem unreasonable. I am using
figures for an average apartment. A home purchase, you can expect
close to $600 (or less) for home loan, $150 for electric, $40 to $150
for phone, cable can be $100 to $170, gas approx. $100, food for

$350 to $450, and the rest you can budget out. Grand total (low to high): $1,340 to $1,620

With these figures add an additional amount from $400 to $600 to include car payment, or other monthly needs or wants. So, $1,740 to $2,220, or $435 a week take home to $555, which means $11 to $14 an hour pay.

This is why joint incomes came into being; one-home incomes began to take a toll on households. People struggled to make ends meet. Except, another problem arose. Extra money meant extra-*unnecessary* spending or unwise decisions. The major problem that came into being is they relied on, let's say, a $16-hour income (2 people times $8 an hour). If one lost their job and they had a car payment that a single, $8-an-hour job would not sustain, they went in the red quickly. Stay true to a one-income household and consider the extra money (pay) as a savings, or a bonus. Never use the extra as income to use for big purchases: home or car. You could regret it later.

NOTES